cooking with

Anne

Kirkmyer

Food photography by
Erin Kassel and Steve Kancianic

Summer Duck Books, LLC

Summer Duck Books, LLC

ISBN: 1480080861
ISBN-13: 9781480080867

This book is dedicated to my dear friend, Sandy Lesberg -

For without your gentle prodding and encouragement-

your knowledge and wisdom,

this book would have never grown wings

Merci, Bon Ami !

thank you

- to my daughter, Erin Kassel, whose creative eye amazed me

- to Mezzeret Crockett, whose faith and friendship kept me encouraged to carry on

- to Peggy and Dudley Patteson for giving me the freedom and the wonderful venue to express my passion

- to my son Claiborne for just being proud

- to my family for not laughing at me

notable notes

- the flour is always all purpose flour

- the salt used in the recipes is kosher salt or sea salt

- the pepper used in the recipes is fresh ground, usually coarsely

- "sprayed" pan or dish refers to spraying the pan with "Pam" or a like product

- a mandoline is a kitchen tool used to thinly slice vegetables

- a "rockfish" is more commonly known as a striped bass

- all oven temperatures are for a conventional oven. if using a convection oven, lower temperature by 25°

- Cavender's Greek Seasoning is a seasoning mixture found in the spice section of your grocery store. It comes with or without MSG.

- the referred mesclun mix can be store-bought or make your own from a variety of young lettuces and herbs

- olive oil is always extra virgin

- the referred bouillon paste or base is a product I use called "Better than Bouillon" - found in the soup section of your grocery store

the referred baking mix is a complete baking mix i.e. Bisquick or Jiffy

- the grits used are "quick cooking" grits

Introduction

about me –

I returned to my home town – the tiny village of Irvington, Virginia – after years of traveling the world. Having lived in Panama and Hawaii, worked as a freelance chef aboard yachts in the Caribbean, moved up and down the Eastern Seaboard as a private chef, and traveled several times to Paris and Europe to continue my culinary education. I have finally come home - where I am now the executive chef at the Hope and Glory Inn - a luxurious country inn - where we offer a most unique dining experience. It is a showcase of our local iconic seafood from the Chesapeake Bay and surrounding rivers. It is here that the idea of writing this book came from a friend who watched me intently as patrons would ask for a recipe and I would race back to the kitchen, scribble the recipe on a piece of paper towel or a store receipt and return to hand it to the beaming patron. "Write a book, offering your recipes in it and you won't have to do this several times each evening." she suggested. Voila! What insight!

my philosophy -

I am a huge Jamie Oliver fan (a.k.a. The Naked Chef)
I love and admire his vibrance - his verve - his methods. The way he strips down a recipe to something basic and beautiful. No culinary jargon or complicated time consuming, meticulous process -- He is my hero!!
That said, my method and philosophy is to cook simply and straight forward using the goal of ultimate flavor to be my guide. Food should be feisty and flavorful. Food should be an adventure for your palate and a sanctuary for your soul. I like to envision the excitement my finished dish will bring to one's taste senses and go backwards from there.
The only way to get to ultimate flavor is to experiment and evolve. Use recipes as a guide but by all means, break away into your own direction. If you don't have an ingredient, substitute something you think will work and then move forward.
Have fun - enjoy - evolve and excite

anne kirkmyer

CONTENTS

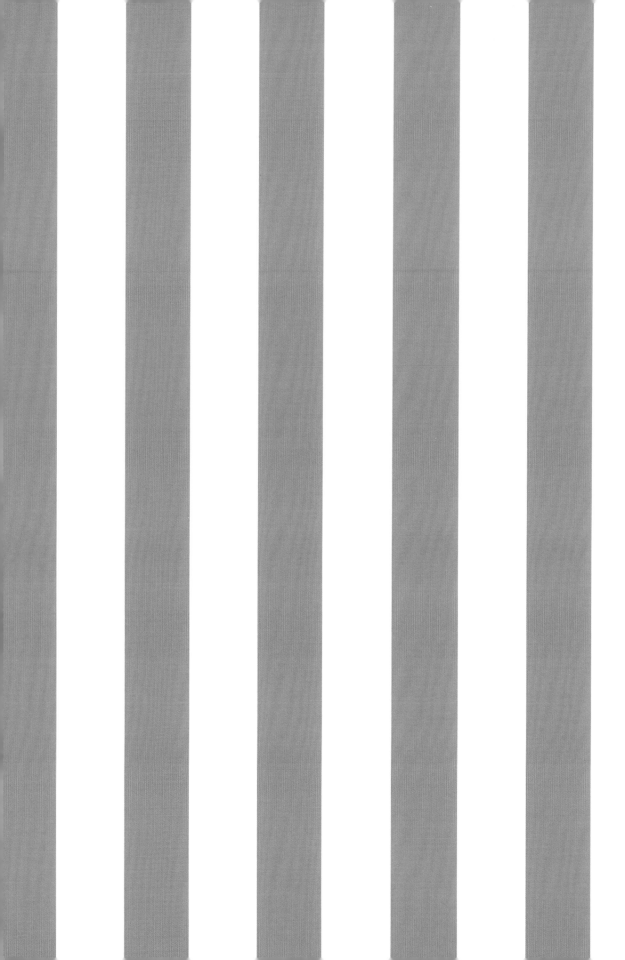

Appetizers

Shrimp Stuffed Baby Portobellos topped with Romano Cheese and Basil Pesto

∽

Serves 4

Who doesn't love the combination of mushrooms, shrimp and cheese?

20 baby portabello mushrooms - 1 to 2 inches in diameter
4 tablespoons butter - softened
8 ounces goat cheese
1 tablespoon dried Italian herbs
1 1/2 cups cooked shrimp - chopped coarsely
1/4 cup green onion - chopped
salt and pepper to taste
1/4 cup basil pesto - fresh or jarred
2 cups Romano cheese - grated
Baby Arugula Salad - recipe follows

Preheat to 350°
After wiping the mushrooms clean with a damp paper towel,
rub them with butter and place them on baking sheet.
Combine goat cheese, dried herbs, shrimp, green onion
and salt and pepper in a small bowl and mix.
Stuff the mushrooms with shrimp mixture. Top 1
teaspoon of pesto and a tablespoon of cheese.
Bake for 15 to 20 minutes.

To serve: Place five mushrooms in a circle on a small plate. Pile a
small mound of arugula salad in the middle of the circle.

Baby Arugula Salad

1/2 cup olive oil
1/4 cup balsamic vinegar
1 teaspoon Cavender's Greek seasoning
2 cups baby arugula

Mix olive oil, vinegar, and Greek seasoning in a jar - shake
vigorously. Toss arugula with appropriate amount of dressing.

Shrimp Stuffed Baby Portobellos topped with Romano Cheese and Basil Pesto

Provincial Mussels with Asiago Toast

∾

Serves 4

The Asiago Toast is to be used for sopping up all the savory broth after the mussels are gone!

6 cloves garlic - minced
6 tablespoons butter
5 dozen mussels - scrubbed
2 cups white wine
salt and pepper
chop parsley
Asiago toast - recipe to follow

In a Dutch oven, sauté garlic and butter for 30 seconds.
Add mussels and cook for another 30 seconds.
Add wine, cover and cook (about 3 to 5 minutes), shaking the pan occasionally, until all the mussels are open.

To serve: Spoon mussels into a soup bowl. Top with an Asiago toast and sprinkle with chopped parsley.

Asiago Toast

4 thick slices of French bread - buttered
3/4 cup of finely grated Asiago cheese

Top French bread with cheese and broil until toasty and bubbly.

Provincial Mussels with Asiago Toast

Oysters a la Joe

◠

Serves 4

*This was my father's favorite way to serve oysters - it has all
the elements men love; cheese, bacon and Tabasco!*

24 shucked oysters on the half shell
salt-and-pepper
6 strips of bacon - cut into 1 inch pieces and cooked until almost crisp
2 cups grated Vermont white cheddar cheese
Tabasco sauce
1/4 cup chopped chives

Preheat to 375°
Place oysters on a baking pan. Sprinkle with salt and pepper. Top each
oyster with a piece of bacon, and two tablespoons of cheese. Dot with 2
to 3 drops of Tabasco. Bake for 10 minutes or until oyster edges curl.

To serve: Place six oysters on a plate and sprinkle with chives.

Creamy Rappahannock Oysters and Exotic Mushrooms in a Puff Pastry Shell

∽

Serves 4

This is a wonderful way to showcase our acclaimed Rappahannock Mollusk

4 Frozen Puff Pastry Shells
2 tablespoons butter
1 tablespoons flour
1 cup cream
1/4 cup fish stock or clam juice
1 teaspoon ground rosemary
1 teaspoon ground thyme
salt and pepper
16-20 shucked oysters - depending on size
2 cups coursley chopped and slightly sauteed assorted mushrooms
(cremini,oyster,potabellas,shitake,chanterelles etc.
thyme sprigs

Prepare puff pastry shells according to directions. Set aside.
In a medium skillet, melt butter over medium heat and stir in flour - whisk until incorporated. Slowly add cream while whisking and cook until smooth, thick and bubbly. Add the fish stock, herbs and salt and pepper. Add oysters and continue to cook and stir until edges of oysters begin to curl - add mushrooms and cook just until heated through. Adjust seasoning.

To serve: Spoon creamed oyster mixture into prepared
puff pastry shell and garnish with a thyme sprig.

Jumbo Lump Crab Dip with Naan Bread Triangles

◞◟

Serves 4

*I serve this rich dip in individual casserole dishes for dipping
with crispy, chewy Indian flatbread triangles*

8 ounces cream cheese - cut into pieces
1/2 cup cream
1/4 cup chopped green onions - green tops included
3 tablespoons capers
2 tablespoons dry sherry
1 teaspoon Old Bay seasoning
dash of Tabasco sauce
1 lb. jumbo lump crab meat
2 cups Vermont cheddar cheese - grated
1/4 teaspoon smoked paprika
chopped parsley for garnish
Naan Bread Triangles - recipe to follow

Preheat to 400°
In a medium saucepan over medium heat, combine the cream and
the cream cheese. Whisk until smooth and hot. Add green onions,
capers, sherry, Old Bay, and Tabasco - continue to stir until well
incorporated. Remove from heat. Gently fold in crab meat.
Spoon mixture into individual sprayed ramekins. Top with cheese and sprinkle
with smoked paprika. Bake for 15 to 20 minutes until hot and bubbly.

To serve: Place ramekin on a small plate. Surround with
Naan bread triangles and garnish with parsley.

Naan Bread Triangles

2 packages Naan Bread - cut into 2 inch triangles
(Naan bread is an Indian flatbread sometimes called Tandoori
bread - Pita bread may be substituted if needed)
1/4 cup olive oil

Preheat to 400°
Place triangles on baking sheet and brush with olive oil. Bake for 5
to 10 minutes until just crispy. Serve immediately with crab dip.

Mini Corn Souflee topped with Jumbo Lump Crab and Proscuitto

∽

Serves 4

The blend of sweet and salty plus the different textures of this dish really makes it work

6 tablespoons butter
1 cup fresh corn
1/2 package corn muffin mix
1/2 cup sour cream
2 tablespoons melted butter
1 tablespoon sugar
1 teaspoon lime juice
1/2 lb. jumbo lump crab
4 tablespoons honey
4 slices thin prosciutto-cut into julienne strips

Preheat 375°
In a skillet, melt the butter and sauté the corn for 5 to 8 minutes. Set aside.
In a bowl stir together corn muffin mix, sour cream, melted butter and sugar. Add corn and mix well. Pour into sprayed single serving ramekins and bake for 20 to 25 minutes until center is set.
In a small bowl, mix lime juice and honey. Set aside.
In a small skillet, sauté crab with four tablespoons butter. Salt and pepper to taste.
On a plate, put the prosciutto and microwave for 7 to 10 minutes until just crispy.

To assemble: On a small plate, spoon one tablespoon of lime honey. Run a knife around corn soufflé and invert - place onto honey pool - top with sautéed crab and frizzeled prosciutto.

Mini Corn Souflee topped with Jumbo Lump Crab and Proscuitto

Tempura Fried Oyster Cocktail with Wasabi Drizzle

∞

Serves 4

*The delicate batter and the kicky wasabi sauce bring this fried oyster
to a new dimension!*

4 cups frying oil
20 raw oysters - drained and patted dry
2 cups tempura batter mix - found in the Asian section a grocery store - mix
according to directions
2 tablespoons wasabi powder
3 tablespoons water
1/4 cup sour cream
2 cups leafy lettuce - cut into julienne strips
lemon wedges

In a wok, deep saucepan or deep fryer bring oil to 350°
Dip oysters into batter and fry until golden - drain well on paper towels.
Mix wasabi powder and water to make a paste and whisk it into the sour
cream. Spoon mixture into a squirt bottle and refrigerate until needed.

To assemble: Fill a martini glass half way with shredded lettuce. Top with
fried oysters and squiggle with wasabi. Garnish with lemon wedges.

Spicy "She" Deviled Crab

Glorified Oysters

~

Serves 4

This is my version of Oysters Rockefeller - my most requested recipe!

24 oysters - shucked
1 tablespoon kosher salt
1/2 cup fresh pesto - recipe to follow
Tabasco sauce
2 cups grated Asiago cheese
chopped parsley for garnish

Preheat to 400°
Place shucked oysters on a baking sheet. Sprinkle each oyster with
a little kosher salt. Dot each oyster with 1/2 tablespoon of pesto
and a drop of Tabasco. Top with 2 tablespoons grated cheese.
Bake for 8 to 10 minutes until oyster edges are beginning to curl.

To Serve: Place six oysters on a plate and sprinkle with parsley.

Pesto

2 cups fresh basil leaves
3 tablespoons pine nuts
3 cloves garlic - smashed and minced
1/2 cup olive oil
1/2 cup grated Parmesan cheese
salt-and-pepper

Combine basil, pine nuts, and garlic in a food processor. Whir
for a few seconds. Add the olive oil - Whir until blended. Add
cheese and pulse again. Salt and pepper to taste.

Glorified Oysters

Ya-Ya Oysters

∾

Serves 4

The unusual aspect to these oysters is the deconstructed ketchup topping

One large can of diced tomatoes - drained
2 tablespoons olive oil
1/2 teaspoon liquid smoke
salt and pepper
3 tablespoons finely chopped red onions
3 teaspoons finely chopped jalapenos
2 tablespoon chopped cilantro
24 shucked oysters on the half shell
2 teaspoons chili oil

Preheat to 250°
Spread tomatoes on baking sheet and toss with olive
oil, salt-and-pepper, and liquid smoke.
Baked 40 to 50 minutes.
Place tomatoes, onions, jalapenos, and cilantro in a
food processor and whir briefly to combine.
Preheat to 350°
Place oysters on baking sheet. Top each oyster with one tablespoon of
tomato mixture and bake 8 to 10 minutes - until edges begin to curl.

To serve: Drizzle top of each oyster with chili oil and garnish with cilantro leaf.

SOUPS

Wild Mushroom Bisque with Parmesan Wafer

 ∾

Serves 4

This is a quick but elegant starter to any meal

3 cups coarsely chopped assorted mushrooms - shiitake, oyster, potabellas etc.
1/4 cup finely chopped shallots
4 tablespoons butter
2 teaspoons beef base paste or 1/4 cup beef stock
2 cups heavy cream
2 tablespoons dry sherry
4 Parmesan wafers - recipe to follow

In a medium saucepan over medium heat, sauté shallots and
mushrooms in the butter just long enough for mushrooms sweat.
Add beef base and stir into mushroom juice until incorporated.
Stir in cream. Increase heat to high and bring to a boil -
allow to reduce for three to four minutes. Remove from
heat. Add sherry to finish. Serve with Parmesan wafer.

Parmesan Wafers

2 cups coarsely grated Parmesan cheese

On a hot griddle or skillet sprinkle 1/4 cup Parmesan cheese in a 2' circle. Allow
to melt and edges begin to brown - turn and let other side cook until golden.

Wild Mushroom Bisque with Parmesan Wafer

Chesapeake Bay Bounty Gumbo

Serves 4

This hearty Louisiana classic is chock-full of goodies from the Chesapeake Bay!

4 tablespoons flour
4 tablespoons butter
2 cups clam stock or fish stock
2 tablespoons Worcestershire sauce
1 teaspoon Tabasco sauce
1 cup Bloody Mary Mix
4 tablespoons olive oil
1 cup coarsely chopped yellow and orange peppers
1 cup coarsely chopped onions
1 cup coarsely chopped celery
4 cloves garlic - smashed and minced
1/2 cup dry white wine
1 14 ounce can diced tomatoes with juice
2 tablespoons chopped fresh thyme
2 teaspoons ground oregano
1 tablespoon dry Italian herbs
1 tablespoon Old Bay Seasoning
salt and pepper
16 shucked oysters
16 Jumbo shrimp - raw and and cleaned
1/2 pound jumbo lump crab meat
2 cups hot cooked rice
Thyme and Parsley for garnish

In a large pot or skillet over medium heat, melt butter
and whisk in flour until well incorporated.
Add one half of clam stock and whisk until thickened, continue
to add stock and whisking until thick and smooth.
Add Worcestershire sauce, Tabasco sauce, and Bloody Mary mix to thick
roux. Continue cooking and whisking until well incorporated.
In a separate skillet, sauté vegetables in the olive oil until just soft but still crisp.
Add minced garlic and cook 30 seconds.
Deglaze pan with white wine. Add tomatoes and juice and let
reduce for two minutes. Add herbs and stir. Adjust seasonings.
Add vegetable mixture to roux mixture and stir to mix.
Add oysters and shrimp and allow to cook until oysters began
to curl and shrimp begins to turn pink. Add crabmeat gently
so as not to break up lumps. Cook until heated through.

To serve: In a soup plate or bowl, place one half cup of hot
cooked rice and gently spoon Gumbo over and around the rice
mound. Garnish with thyme sprig and chopped parsley.

Creamy Tomato Soup With Pesto

Serves 4

So easy to prepare - and so pretty to look at!

2 tablespoons olive oil
1/4 cup shallots - minced
2 cloves garlic - smashed and minced
6 cups Italian plum tomatoes - cut into chunks and drained
1 cup chicken stock
4 tablespoons butter
1/2 cup heavy cream
1 teaspoon Cavender's Greek season
salt and pepper
1/4 cup sour cream
1/4 cup pesto - fresh or jarred

In a medium saucepan over medium heat, sauté
shallots and garlic in the olive oil.
Put tomatoes into food processor and pulse until blended. Add tomatoes,
chicken stock, and butter to saucepan . Simmer for 30 minutes
Add cream and stir. Add seasonings - adjust to taste.

To Serve: Ladle soup into soup bowls and garnish
with sour cream and pesto squiggles.

Tip: An easy way to make squiggles - spoon the sour cream
into the corner of a small zip lock bag, clip corner with
scissors and squeeze to squiggle. Repeat with pesto.

Oven Roasted Vegetable Soup

⁓

Serves 4

At the end of the week, my grandmother would make what she would call "clean out the refrigerator soup" - this soup reminds me fondly of that very soup!

2 cups diced tomatoes - drained
1/2 cup olive oil
salt and pepper
1 cup red onions - 1/2 inch dice
1 cup celery - sliced
1 cup baby carrots - sliced
1 cup beets -1/2 inch dice
1 cup zucchini -1/2 inch dice
1 tablespoon dried Italian herbs
2 cups shredded cabbage
4 cups vegetable stock

Preheat 300°
Toss tomatoes with 4 tablespoons of olive oil,salt and pepper. Spread on baking sheet and roast in the oven for 30 - 45 mins. Remove and increase temperature to 425°. On another baking sheet; toss onions, celery, carrots, beets, and zucchini with remaining olive oil, salt and pepper, and dried Italian herbs. Roast for 10-15 minutes until tender. In the final 4 to 5 minutes of cooking, toss in cabbage.
In a medium saucepan, heat stock to boiling. Add tomatoes and vegetables - lower to simmer for five minutes. Adjust seasonings to taste.

Summer Cucumber and Crab Soup

ᐰ

Serves 4

Refreshing, cool, and scrumptious

3 seedless cucumbers - peeled and cut into chunks
1 yellow pepper - cut into chunks
5 green onions - chopped coarsely
2 cloves garlic - smash and minced
1 tablespoon chopped cilantro
2 cups Greek yogurt
2 cups sour cream
salt-and-pepper
1/8 teaspoon chipotle chili powder
4 five ounce servings crab salad - recipe to follow
paprika

Place cucumbers, peppers, onions, garlic, cilantro, yogurt and
sour cream in food processor and whir until smooth.
Strain through a colander and stir in seasonings. Refrigerate.

To Serve: Place a small mound of crab salad in a soup plate and gently ladle
cucumber soup around the crab. Garnish with paprika and cilantro leaves.

Crab Salad

1 lb. jumbo lump crab
4 tablespoons mayonnaise
3 tablespoons finely chopped red onion
4 tablespoons finely chopped celery
1 tablespoon lemon juice
3 tablespoons capers
1/2 teaspoon Old Bay Seasoning
salt and pepper to taste

Combine all ingredients.

Summer Cucumber and Crab Soup

Sweet Summer Corn Bisque with Smithfield Ham

༄

Serves 4

The sweetness of the summer corn and the saltiness of the ham blend harmoniously in this creamy soup

6 cups white corn - cut off the cob
4 tablespoons butter
1 tablespoon sugar
1 teaspoon cumin
2 tablespoons chopped shallots
1 1/2 cup chicken stock
2 cups heavy cream
salt-and-pepper
4 thin slices Smithfield or country ham - cut in julienne strips
1/4 teaspoon smoked paprika

In a medium skillet over medium heat, sauté the corn in the butter for 3-4 minutes. Add sugar, cumin and shallots and sauté another three minutes. Deglaze pan with chicken stock and allow to simmer for three minutes. Remove from heat and allow to cool slightly. Pour into a food processor and whir for about two minutes. Strain and press through a fine sieve into a saucepan. Over medium heat, add cream and allow to reduce until thick - about 10 minutes. Season to taste with salt and pepper. Put the strips of ham on a plate and microwave until hot and slightly crispy.

To Serve: Ladle soup into soup bowl - top with crispy ham strips and garnish with smoked paprika.

Rappahannock Oyster Stew

Serves 4

In our neck of the woods - oyster stew is traditionally served at the holidays. This version is thick and creamy and brimful of our famous Rappahanock oysters.

1/2 stick butter
1/4 finely chopped shallots
1 clove garlic - smashed and minced
3 tablespoons flour
1 can evaporated milk
3 cups heavy cream
1 tablespoon Worcestershire sauce
1 teaspoon Old Bay seasoning
2 tablespoons fish bouillon paste
1 pint oysters - drained
salt and pepper
chopped parsley
paprika

In a medium skillet or saucepan melt the butter and sauté shallots, add the garlic. Sprinkle with flour and whisk to incorporate. Slowly add the evaporated milk, and the cream, whisking until slightly thick. Add Worcestershire, Old Bay and fish bouillon - continuing to stir until thick and creamy. Add oysters and simmer until edges began to curl. Salt and pepper to taste.

To serve: Ladle stew into soup plates and garnish
with chopped parsley and paprika.

Garden Bounty Gazpacho with Shrimp and Avocado

∾

Serves 4

We serve this soup as a "salad in a soup bowl" during the summer when our beautiful heirloom tomatoes are in season

1 1/2 cups tomato juice
1/2 cup vegetable stock
2 tablespoons Worcestershire sauce
1/2 teaspoon Old Bay seasoning
2 cloves garlic - smashed and minced
1/4 teaspoon Tabasco sauce
1/2 cup chopped onions
2 cups peeled and chopped cucumbers
2 cups chopped tomatoes
3/4 cup chopped yellow peppers
20 medium cooked shrimp
1/2 cup chopped avocado
16 croutons - recipe to follow
chopped cilantro for garnish

Except for shrimp, avocado, and cilantro - combine all ingredients in a bowl and chill for several hours.

To serve: Ladle gazpacho into chilled soup plates and garnish with avocado and shrimp - sprinkle with chopped cilantro. Place four croutons around edge of soup.

Croutons

4 one inch thick slices of French bread - cut into 1" cubes
2 tablespoons olive oil
1/2 teaspoon Cavender's Greek Seasoning

Preheat to 350°
Toss bread cubes with olive oil and Greek Seasoning. Spread on baking
sheet and bake in oven until golden and crispy - about 15 minutes.

Garden Bounty Gazpacho with Shrimp and Avacado

Savory Sweet Potato Soup

∾

Serves 4

This is a great soup to serve after the holidays - using your left over sweet potatoes !

4 cups of cooked and mashed sweet potatoes
1/4 cup maple syrup
1 cup heavy cream
1/2 cup diced tomatoes - drained
1 cup chicken stock
1/4 cup vindaloo sauce (an Indian curry sauce found in the international section of fine grocery stores)
1/4 cup plain yogurt

Combine sweet potatoes, syrup, and cream in a food processor and whir until well blended. Put into a saucepan over low heat and allow to simmer. Put tomatoes into a food processor and whir quickly until just smooth - add to soup along with chicken stock. Stir in vindaloo sauce and whisk until well incorporated and soup is hot.

To serve: Ladle into soup plate and garnish with yogurt squiggle.

Savory Sweet Potato Soup

Crab Bisque with a Puffed Asiago Twist

Serves 4

Crab Bisque is a classic on the Chesapeake Bay - thick and laden with jumbo lump crab - its everybody's favorite!

2 tablespoons flour
4 tablespoon butter
1 cup lobster bouillon -(1 tablespoon Better than Bouillon Lobster base to one cup boiling water) Fish stock or Clam juice may be used
2 1/2 cups cream
salt and pepper
1/2 lb. jumbo lump crabmeat
1 teaspoon paprika
4 Asiago Twists - recipe to follow
4 oz. dry sherry- slightly warmed in microwave

In a medium sauce pan over medium heat, melt butter and whisk in flour to make a blonde roux. Add bouillon and whisk until thick and bubbly - add cream a little at a time - stirring until smooth and creamy. Adjust seasoning to taste. Gently fold in crabmeat and continue to cook just until crab is hot.

To serve: Ladle crab bisque into soup plates or bowls. Sprinkle with paprika and lay an Asiago Twist across bowl. Accompany soup bowl with a shot glass of warm sherry to added at diner's discretion.

Puffed Asiago Twists

1 frozen puff pastry sheet
3 tablespoons Asiago (parmesan or romano) cheese - finely grated

Pre-heat to 350 degrees. Lay puff pastry sheet on cutting surface. Sprinkle with grated cheese - cut into strips 3/4 " wide x 8" long. Holding both ends of strip, twist slightly so strip takes on a twisty look. Place on a sprayed baking sheet and bake until puffy and golden - 8-10 mins.

Crab Bisque

Rockfish And Potato Chowder

∾

Serves 4

*This hearty chowder makes a great light autumn dinner
paired with a salad and some crusty bread*

8 tablespoons butter
1/3 cup flour
2 cups fish stock or clam juice
2 cups cream
1 cup chopped onions
1 cup chopped celery
2 cloves garlic - smashed and minced
1 Rockfish fillet - skinned (or any whitefish) and cut into 3/4" cubes - about 2 cups
1 1/2 cups cooked red skin potatoes - cubed and cooked fork tender
1 teaspoon old Bay seasoning
2 tablespoons Worcestershire sauce
salt-and-pepper

In a medium saucepan over medium heat, melt 4 tablespoons of butter and whisk in flour. Slowly add the fish stock, whisking until thick. Add cream and stir until thick and creamy. Set aside.
In a medium skillet over medium heat, melt remaining 4 tablespoons of butter. Sauté onions and celery until cooked still crisp - add garlic and fish cubes. Cook until just fish is just white and opaque.
Combine cream base with fish and vegetable mixture. Add more cream or stock if needed to thin. Stir in potatoes, Old Bay seasoning, and Worcestershire. Salt and pepper to taste. Simmer for 8 to 10 mins. and serve.

Salads

Cucumber Round Salad with A Creamy Lemon Pepper Dressing

Serves 4

This salad makes an elegant and stunning presentation

1 long English seedless cucumber
4 cups mesclun mix
1 cup Creamy Lemon Pepper Dressing - recipe to follow
1/4 cup finely shredded carrots
2 shallots - mandolined and separated into rings
8 grape tomatoes - cut in quarters
2 tablespoons chopped parsley

With a mandoline - cut 4 long, unbroken, horizontal cucumber slices.
Set aside.

To serve: Form a round with cucumber slice in the middle of a salad plate.
Toss the mesculin with the appropriate amount of dressing and place
one serving inside the cucumber round. Top with carrots and shallots.
Sprinkle tomatoes and chopped parsley around perimeter of plate.

Creamy Lemon Pepper Dressing

1 tin of anchovies
2 cloves of garlic, smashed and minced
3 tablespoons lemon juice
2 tablespoons mayonnaise
1 teaspoon tarragon
1/2 cup olive oil
1 tablespoon course ground pepper

In a food processor - combine anchovies, garlic, lemon juice, mayonnaise, and tarragon. Whir until blended and slowly add olive oil in a slow and steady stream until thick and creamy. Stir in pepper.

Cucumber Round Salad with Creamy Lemon Pepper Dressing

Mache and Strawberry Salad with Herb Goat Cheese and Pomegranate Vinaigrette

༄

Serves 4

This sweet and savory combination looks just as delectable as it tastes

9 ounces mache, otherwise known as lambs lettuce
8-10 strawberries - cut into quarters
1/2 cup balsamic vinegar
1 tablespoon honey
1/2 cup olive oil
2 tablespoons pomegranate molasses - found in Asian markets
2 teaspoons Cavender's Greek seasoning
2 ounces pine nuts
3 ounces goat cheese mixed with 1 teaspoon dry Italian herbs

Place strawberries in a bowl with 4 tablespoons of balsamic vinegar
and the honey. Mix well and refrigerate for one hour or more.
Mix remaining balsamic vinegar with olive oil, the pomegranate molasses
and the Greek season in a squirt bottle. Shake well and refrigerate.

To serve: In a bowl, mix mache with appropriate amount of dressing and toss.
Pile high on the salad plate - adorn with marinated
strawberries, crumbled goat cheese and pine nuts.

Sweet Summer Corn Relish

∾

Serves 4

A great accompaniment for any backyard barbecue

4 cups white corn - cut off the cob
1/2 cup olive oil
1/4 cup red wine vinegar
2 cloves garlic - smashed and minced
1 teaspoon cumin powder
2 teaspoons Cavender's Greek seasoning
1/4 cup chopped cilantro
1 can black beans - rinsed and drained
1/4 cup chopped sweet/hot peppers (found in pickle section of grocery store)
1 cup chopped tomatoes
2 tablespoons lime juice
salt and pepper
4 Boston Lettuce cups

In a medium skillet over medium heat sauté corn in two tablespoons
olive oil for 8-10 mins. Salt and pepper to taste Transfer to a bowl.
In a jar combine olive oil, red wine vinegar, garlic, cumin,
and Greek season. Shake well. Set aside.
To corn, add cilantro, black beans, peppers, tomatoes, and lime juice. Mix well.
Pour jarred dressing over corn mixture and allow to marinate
for several hours. Salt and pepper to taste.

To serve: Spoon corn relish into Boston lettuce
cup and garnish with cilantro leaves.

Apple Blossom Salad with Apple Cider and Honey Dressing

∽

Serves 4

The marriage of stilton cheese and crisp apples brings ever loving bliss to this salad!

6 cups mesclun mix
apple cider dressing - recipe to follow
2 granny smith apples - peeled, quartered, (core and seed section cut away) and cut into thin slices
1/4 teaspoon smoked paprika
1/3 cup stilton cheese or other good blue vein cheese
1/4 cup craisins or dried cherries
4 tablespoons shelled pistachios

In a bowl, toss the mesclun with enough dressing to coat evenly. Pile mesclun on a salad plate. Arrange the slices of apples in an overlapped circle on top of the salad to resemble a flower. Sprinkle lightly with smoked paprika. Sprinkle with cheese and distribute craisins and pistachios around edge of plate.

Apple Cider Dressing

2/3 cup olive oil
1/4 cup apple cider vinegar
3 tablespoon honey
1 teaspoon Cavender Greek Seasoning

Combine all ingredients in a jar or squirt bottle and shake well.

Apple Blossom Salad with Apple Cider and Honey Dressing

Grilled Pear Salad with Herbed Goat Cheese, Candied Pecans, Dried Blueberries, and a Peach Balsamic Dressing

Serves 4

This salad has all the promise of an early fall and the lingering of late summer

2 red pears (or any ripe pear) cut into medium slices (6 - 8 slices per salad)
8 cups mesclun mix
peach balsamic dressing - recipe to follow
1/2 cup herb goat cheese - recipe to follow
1 cup candied pecans - recipe to follow
1/2 cup dried blueberries

Pre-heat grill or grill pan. Place pear slices on hot grill just long enough to mark the pear with grill marks. Do not over cook. Remove and set aside.
Toss balsamic dressing with mesclun.

To serve: Place dressed mesclun mix on salad plate. Top with pear slices. Sprinkle with herb goat cheese. Place pecans and blueberries around edge.

Candied Pecans

2 cups whole pecans
2 tablespoons orange juice
1/2 cup light brown sugar
1 teaspoon cumin
dash of cayenne pepper

Pre-heat to 375 degrees. Combine all ingredients - mix well and spread evenly on pan. Bake for 8-10 mins until bubbly. Transfer to a piece of foil that has been sprayed - spreading and separating as you transfer. Allow to cool and harden.

Herb Goat Cheese

4 oz. goat cheese
1 1/2 teaspoon dried Italian herbs
1 teaspoon Cavenders Greek Seasoning

Place ingredients in a small bowl and mix well.

Balsamic Vinaigrette

1/2 olive oil
1/4 cup flavored balsamic - peach is best for this recipe
1/4 teaspoon each - salt and pepper

Put all ingredients in a jar and shake well.
Refridgerate for a few hours before use.

Wedge of Romaine with Tiny Tim Tomatoes, Mandolined Onions, Crispy Bacon and Blue Cheese Dressing

Serves 4

This is a take on the old wedge of iceberg salad so popular in the 60s - no matter how you slice it - it is still great!

1 large head Romaine lettuce - cut into four wedges
1 pint of Tiny Tim Tomatoes - cut in halves
1/4 red onion - mandolined into super thin slices
6 slices crisp bacon - crumbled
1 cup Gorgonzola dressing - recipe to follow
1/4 teaspoon smoked paprika

Place wedge of Romaine on salad plate and scatter with tomatoes and bacon bits. Top with mandolined red onions. Dollop generously with dressing and sprinkle with smoked paprika.

Gorgonzola Dressing

1 cup sour cream
1/4 cup heavy cream
1 cup crumbled Gorgonzola cheese
3 tablespoons red wine vinegar
salt and pepper

Put all ingredients into food processor and whir until blended still chunky. Refrigerate until needed.

Tower Beet Salad with Fig Balsamic Dressing

∽

Serves 4

This salad will get your dinner party started impressively -- have your local hardware store cut you four sections of PVC pipe that measure 2 1/2" wide by 3" tall

4 large fresh beets - (canned beets can be used)
2 yellow peppers cut into 1/2" cubes
2 tablespoons olive oil
3/4 cup fig balsamic dressing - recipe to follow
salt and pepper
5 ounces mache or arugula
4 ounces herbed goat cheese - recipe to follow
4 tablespoons shelled pistachio nuts
chopped chives

Preheat to 400°
Wrap beets in foil and roast in hot oven for one hour or until fork tender. Unwrapped and slip skins off while still warm. Allow to cool.
Put chopped peppers on baking sheet and toss with olive oil. Roast in hot oven or 10 minutes. Remove and allow to cool.
Chop cooled beets into 1/2" cubes. Put into a small bowl and add three tablespoons fig dressing, salt and pepper and toss.
Put peppers into a separate small bowl and add two tablespoons fig dressing, salt and pepper and toss.
Put greens in a bowl and toss with four tablespoons of the dressing. Salt and pepper to taste.

To assemble: Wash and then stand three-inch PVC pipe on a salad plate. Spoon 1/4 of the beets into the pipe and packed down with fingertips. Spoon two tablespoons of the herb goat cheese into pipe. Pack gently with fingertips. Top with 1/4 of the peppers - pack well. Place in refrigerator until needed.

To serve: Lift PVC pipe up and away as you press down with fingertips on vegetable mixture. Pile dressed greens on top of the tower and sprinkle pistachios and chopped chives around perimeter of plate. Dot with more dressing.

Fig Balsamic Dressing

3/4 cup olive oil
1/3 cup fig balsamic vinegar
1 tablespoon Cavender's Greek seasoning

Combine all ingredients in a jar and shake well.

Herb Goat Cheese

6 ounces goat cheese
2 tablespoons finely chopped shallots
1 tablespoon dried Italian herbs

In a small bowl, combine all until well mixed.

Tower Beet Salad

Chopped Salad with Classic Green Goddess Dressing

Serves 4

*Remember Green Goddess dressing from the 70s - it's back! This is
a fun salad to serve because of the colorful presentation*

4 cups chopped Romaine lettuce
1 cup Green Goddess dressing - recipe to follow
1/4 teaspoon smoked paprika
3/4 cup chopped yellow pepper
1/2 cup chopped red onion
3/4 cup chopped celery
1 cup grated white Vermont cheddar cheese
1 cup frozen petite peas - drained and slightly warmed in microwave
1 cup chopped boiled eggs
12 grape tomatoes - quartered
1/4 cup chopped chives

To Serve: For each serving, place a mound of lettuce in the middle of a salad
plate. Drizzle with two tablespoons of dressing. Sprinkle with smoked paprika.
Surround with small portions of vegetables, cheese, and egg.
Sprinkle chopped chives over all.

Green Goddess Dressing

1 cup mayonnaise
1/2 cup sour cream
1/2 cup chopped green onions
1 tablespoon dried tarragon
1 tablespoon lemon juice
2 tablespoons white wine vinegar
2 tins anchovy filets
2 cloves garlic, smashed and minced
1/2 teaspoon Cavender's Greek Seasoning

Place all ingredients in food processor and blend until smooth and creamy.

Our Classic Caesar Salad

∾

Serves 4

Our Caesar dressing has a punch of anchovies and a smack of fresh lemon!

2 heads Romaine lettuce - crisped and cut into bite size pieces
8 Parmesan cheese slices - shaved with a vegetable peeler - about 3" long
20 French bread croutons - recipe to follow
1/2 cup Caesar dressing - recipe to follow
freshly course ground pepper

Place the lettuce in a chilled bowl - toss well with the dressing. Place a large handful of salad on salad plate. Crisscross two slices of Parmesan on top. Place croutons around edge of salad and top with fresh ground pepper

Caesar dressing

2 tins anchovies with oil
2 cloves garlic - smashed and minced
1/4 cup fresh lemon juice
1/2 cup olive oil

Combine all ingredients(except the olive oil) in a food processor and whir until smooth - while processor is still running, add the olive oil slowly in a steady stream until dressing is thick and creamy.

French Bread Croutons

1 1/2 cups French bread - cut into 3/4" pieces
1/4 cup olive oil
1 teaspoon Cavender's Greek seasoning

Preheat to 300°
Toss bread cubes with olive oil and sprinkle with Greek seasoning
- toss again. Bake until crispy and golden - about 20 minutes.

Watermelon Salad with Feta and Mint Dressing

Serves 4

Refreshing and unusual -- a great dish to serve for a summer picnic dinner

5 cups mesclun mix
1 lb. seedless watermelon - cut into 3/4 inch cubes
1/2 cup mint dressing - recipe to follow
1/2 cup mandolined sweet onion - separated into rings
4 ounces herbed feta cheese - crumbled

In a bowl, combine mesclun mix and watermelon. Toss with mint dressing and garnish with onion rings and feta cheese.

Mint Dressing

1/3 cup balsamic vinegar
3/4 cup olive oil
1 teaspoon Cavender's Greek season
3 tablespoons mint jelly

Combine all in a food processor and whir until blended.

Entrees

Duck Breast with Cherries in Port Wine Sauce

Serves 4

*Although the sauce is superb with cherries - other seasonal
fruit may be used, such as peaches or raspberries*

4 large duck breasts - thawed if frozen
salt and pepper
Port wine sauce with cherries - recipe to follow
rosemary sprigs

In a medium skillet over medium high, sear the breasts - skin side down,
until skin is brown and crispy and fat has been rendered - about 4-5 minutes.
Remove breast from pan and place on baking sheet. Reserve duck drippings.
Remove skin and discard. Sprinkle duck with salt and pepper and roast
in the oven for 8 to 10 minutes. Allow to rest 5 minutes before slicing.

To serve: Slice duck breast thinly and place on plate. Serve
topped with Port wine sauce. Garnish with rosemary sprig.

Port Wine Sauce with Cherries

1 tablespoon reserved duck drippings
2 tablespoons finely chopped shallots
1 cup pitted cherries (frozen may be used)
2/3 cup ruby port
1 tablespoon sugar
1 tablespoon cornstarch mixed with 2 tablespoons water
3 tablespoons butter

In reserved duck drippings, sauté shallots for one minute. Add fruit, and the port wine. Sprinkle in the sugar and stir to incorporate. Bring to a simmer and thicken with cornstarch. Whisk in butter.

**Duck Breast with Cherries in Port Wine Sauce,
Oatmeal Souflee, and Braised Collards**

Chicken Cordon Bleu with Dijonnaise Sauce

∽

Serves 4

We make this in our cooking classes because it is simple and yet classically elegant

4 thin chicken breast cutlets
8 inch slices of deli ham
1 1/2 cups grated cheese - Fontina or Gruyere
2 tablespoons fresh thyme - chopped
salt and pepper
1 1/2 cups Panko breadcrumbs
2 eggs
1 tablespoon water
1/2 cup olive oil
Thyme sprigs
1 cup Dijonnaise Sauce - recipe to follow

Preheat to 350°
Lay chicken breast out and top slices of ham and one fourth
portion of the grated cheese. Leave a half inch margin.
Tuck in the sides of the breast and roll up tight like a jelly
roll. Squeeze tightly to seal or secure with toothpicks.
Mix breadcrumbs with thyme, salt and pepper.
Beat together the eggs and the water. Dip the chicken roll into the egg
mixture and then roll in the breadcrumbs. Continue until all rolls are done.
In a medium skillet, heat the olive oil over medium
heat and brown the rolls lightly.
Transfer to a baking sheet and place in hot oven to finish cooking
for 10 to 15 minutes. Slice each roll on the diagonal.

To Serve: Place a pool of Dijonnaise Sauce onto plate and top
with diagonal slices of chicken. Garnish with thyme sprigs.

Dijonnaise Sauce

1 cup chicken stock
2 cups heavy cream
2 tablespoons Dijon mustard

In a medium saucepan, boil the chicken stock and 1 cup of the cream - allow reduce to half. Add the other cup of cream and allow to continue to reduce - about 30 minutes. When sauce is thick and creamy, whisk in mustard.

Grilled Jumbo Shrimp And Grits

Serves 4

The smokiness of the grilled shrimp lends the full flavor of the Southern classic - but the secret is in the grits!

6 tablespoons butter
1/2 cup chopped onions
1/2 cup chopped yellow peppers
1/2 cup chopped celery
2 cloves garlic - smashed and minced
1/2 cup white wine
2 tablespoons flour
1 cup fish bouillon or clam juice
1 can diced tomatoes - drained
1/2 teaspoon Tabasco or to taste
2 teaspoons lemon juice
2 teaspoons ground oregano
2 teaspoons finely chopped fresh thyme
24 jumbo shrimp - rubbed with olive oil, salt and
pepper and grilled until well marked
4 cups creamy three cheese grits - recipe to follow
fresh thyme sprigs

In a large skillet, over medium heat, melt three tablespoons of butter and sauté vegetables until slightly cooked but still crunchy. Add garlic during last 30 seconds of cooking. Deglaze with wine and simmer for two minutes. Pour into a bowl and set aside.
Putting skillet back on heat, heat remaining butter - sprinkle with flour and whisk until incorporated. Slowly add bouillon while whisking until thick. Add tomatoes, Tabasco, lemon juice, and herbs. Stir to combine. Add shrimp and allow simmer two to three minutes. Correct seasonings.

To serve: Spoon 1 cup creamy grits into soup plate. Top with shrimp mixture and garnish with thyme sprigs.

Creamy Three Cheese Grits

3 cups water
1 cup grits
1 teaspoon salt
4 ounces cream cheese
1 cup Gruyere cheese - grated
2 ounces blue cheese - crumbled
1/4 cup cream
salt and pepper

Boil the water in medium saucepan and add salt. Add grits and stir - reduce heat. Cover and gently simmer for five minutes until thick. Add cream cheese and stir until well incorporated. Add remaining cheeses and stir. Add cream, stir until smooth and creamy. Add salt and pepper according to taste.

Pan Seared Scallops with Buerre Blanc and Mustard-Honey Dapple

∾

Serves 4

A large "dry pack" sea scallop is a must for the success of this dish

16 to 24 large sea scallops at least 1" in diameter
4 tablespoons olive oil
salt and pepper
Buerre Blanc Sauce - recipe to follow
Mustard Honey Sauce - recipe to follow

Rub 2 tablespoons of olive oil over all the scallops and sprinkle liberally with salt and pepper. Put the remaining 2 tablespoons of olive oil in a large sauté pan on high heat. When oil is hot, place the scallops in pan and sear for 1 min. before reducing heat to medium - allow to continue cooking without touching or turning them for 2 mins. Reduce heat to low and turn them over to cook for 2 mins.

To serve: Place 4- 6 scallops on trail of buerre blanc - top each scallop with a dapple of mustard honey sauce. Serve immediatley

Buerre Blanc

1 cup fish stock - (clam juice can be used)
1 cup heavy cream
2 tablespoons butter

Combine stock and cream in a medium saucepan over high heat- until it comes to a boil. Reduce to a vigorous simmer and allow to reduce for 30 to 40 mins. Once it is reduced and very thick, whisk in the butter - add more cream if needed.

Mustard Honey Sauce

3 tablespoons whole-grain mustard
1/2 tablespoon honey

Combine in a small bowl and mix well.

**Pan Seared Scallops with Buerre Blanc and a Tenderloin Medallion
served with Fennel Corn and Roasted Asparagus**

Pan Seared Salmon with Capers, Shallots, and Lemon Sauce served atop Spinach Colcannon

∽

Serves 4

This is a rich and hearty dish from the shores of Ireland

1 1/2 pounds skinless and trimmed salmon fillets - cut into four portions
2 tablespoons olive oil
salt and pepper
Caper, Lemon, and Shallot Sauce - recipe to follow
Spinach Colcannon - recipe to follow
chopped parsley

Score the salmon fillets and rub with olive oil. Sprinkle with salt and pepper. Place in a nonstick pan over medium heat and cook until golden and slightly crispy - about four to five minutes. Pour prepared sauce over fish - remove from heat and cover. Allow to rest for three to four minutes.Salmon will be medium rare.

To Serve: Place a generous dollop of Colcannon on plate. Top with fish and spoon extra sauce around edges. Garnish with chopped parsley.

Caper, Lemon, And Shallot Sauce

1/3 cup fresh lemon juice
1/2 cup olive oil
1 teaspoon Cavender's Greek Seasoning
1/4 cup capers
1/2 thinly sliced shallots
1 tablespoon fresh chopped thyme

Put all ingredients in a large wide mouth jar -
shake vigorously until well blended.

Spinach Colcannon

3 cups prepared hot mashed potatoes
1 cup cooked spinach - warm and patted dry
4 tablespoons butter
salt and pepper

In a bowl, mix potatoes, spinach, and butter. Salt and pepper to taste.

**Pan Seared Salmon with Capers, Shallots, and Lemon
Sauce served atop Spinach Colcannon**

French Countryside Cassoulet

∽

Serves 8 to 10

This recipe requires some prep work the day before -- but the end result is worth the rich flavors of such a decadent "peasant" dish

1 lb. dried navy beans (or great northerns) - canned
beans can be used - drain and rinse beforehand
2 quarts water
2 tablespoons bouillon paste or 4 cubes (beef or vegetable)
salt and pepper
1 5-7 lb. duck - thawed if frozen - cut into pieces i.e. legs, breast, thighs
4 cups olive oil
7 cloves of minced garlic
1 lb. andouille sausage, sliced (or any smoked sausage)
2 lbs. boneless leg of lamb - cut into 1"cubes
2 onions cut into chunks
2 cups white wine
2 14 oz. cans of diced tomatoes - with juice
2 tablespoons fresh or dried thyme
2 tablespoons ground oregano
2 cups fresh breadcrumbs
2 tablespoons olive oil
4 tablespoons chopped parsley

Day Before: Cook the beans in the water with the bouillon - either in a crockpot or on the stovetop - until beans are tender. About two hours. Refrigerate.
Preheat to 250°
Make the duck confit by fitting the cut up duck tightly in a pyrex casserole dish - sprinkle with four cloves of minced garlic and salt and pepper. Cover with 4 cups of olive oil and cover with foil. Put in oven for four to five hours - until meat is fork tender. Allow to cool. Separate bone and skin from meat. Refrigerate meat.

∾

Day Of: Remove duck and beans from refrigerator.
In a large skillet, sauté sliced sausage - set aside.
Sauté the lamb pieces - set aside.
Sauté onion in same pan as meats - deglaze with white wine, and allow to simmer two minutes. Add tomatoes, thyme, oregano, and three minced garlic cloves.
Continue to cook or another minute or so - add beans and stir to combine. Salt and pepper generously.

To Assemble: Preheat to 325°
In a large covered casserole dish, spoon one half of the bean/tomato mixture then top with layers of the sausage, duck, and lamb. Repeat layers as needed. Bake for 1 1/2 hours.
Sauté the breadcrumbs in a skillet until golden - add one tablespoon of parsley.

To Serve: During the last two minutes of cooking - top the Cassoulet with the breadcrumb mixture and allowed to brown a bit.
Serve cassoulet in soup plates with a side of crusty, buttery peasant toast. Garnish with chopped parsley.

Chateaubriand with Roquefort Sauce

∾

Serves 4

How blissful is the marriage of a fine steak and the flavor of a good blue cheese

1 beef tenderloin, trimmed and cleaned
3 tablespoons olive oil
2 tablespoons minced fresh rosemary
2 tablespoons minced fresh thyme
salt and pepper
1/2 cup Roquefort sauce - recipe to follow
fresh rosemary sprigs

Preheat to 400°
Cut out the middle 9 inch section of the tenderloin - this will be your
Chateaubriand. Rub it well the olive oil, rosemary, thyme, salt and pepper.
Roast in hot oven for 20 minutes. Remove and allow to
rest or 10 minutes for slicing. (Beef will be rare)
To Serve: Carve the Chateaubriand in half-inch slices. Drizzle
with Roquefort sauce and garnish with rosemary sprigs.

Roquefort Sauce

2 tablespoons butter
8 ounces Roquefort cheese(or Gorgonzola or Blue Cheese)
2 tablespoon heavy cream

Combine all ingredients in a small saucepan over low
heat - simmer and whisk for two minutes.

Chateaubriand with Roquefort Cream Sauce, Haricots Verts, and Roasted Cauliflower and Baby Carrots

Slow Braised Short Ribs On a Rosemary and Thyme Potato Mash surrounded by a Roasted Root Vegetables

∾

Serves 4

What a satisfying meal on a cold winter night!

12-16 beef short ribs - 3 to 4 per person
salt and pepper
1/4 cup vegetable oil
4 cups beef stock
one bottle of red wine - reserve one cup
1/2 cup flour
1/2 cup water
1 tablespoon Kitchen Bouquet (found in the condiment section of your grocer)
8 to 10 Yukon potatoes - peeled and quartered
4 tablespoons butter
2 tablespoons finely minced rosemary
2 tablespoons finely mixed thyme
salt and pepper
one small bag baby carrots
2 cups cooked beets - cut into 3/4" cubes (canned can be used)
2 cups red onion - coarsely chopped
1/4 cup olive oil
salt and pepper
Rosemary sprigs

Rub beef ribs with salt and pepper. In a Dutch oven browned ribs in oil on all sides. Add beef stock and wine - cover and simmer for three to four hours, until fork tender. Remove ribs and cover to keep warm. Strain remaining wine/stock mixture and return to Dutch oven. Bring to a full boil. Combine flour and water in a jar and shake vigorously.

Slowly whisk flour mixture into boiling wine/stock mixture. Stir until thick and smooth. Add Kitchen Bouquet and reserved cup of wine. Salt and pepper to taste. Return ribs to pot and keep warm.

Place Yukon potatoes into a pot of boiling salted water and cook until fork tender. Drain and mash with masher, adding butter and herbs. Salt and pepper to taste. Preheat to 375°

Toss baby carrots, beets, and onions with olive oil and salt and pepper. Spread on baking sheet and oven roast or 10-15 minutes.

To Serve: In a soup plate - put a generous spoon of herb potatoes. Top with a portion of short ribs and gravy and surround with vegetables. Garnish a rosemary sprigs.

Glory, Glory Crab Cakes with Amen Tartar Sauce

∽

Serves 4

These Crab Cakes get rave reviews every time - the secret is in the Ritz!!

1 lb. jumbo lump crabmeat
2 tablespoons mayonnaise
1 tablespoons lemon juice
1 teaspoon Old Bay Seasoning
salt and pepper
2 Ritz Crackers - crushed

Combine all ingredients in a bowl and mix gently.
Refridgerate for at least two hours.
Pre-heat oven to 350°. Form 8 crab cakes from crab mixture and place on sprayed baking pan. Cover with foil and bake for about 8 - 10 mins. Uncover and allow to brown for another 5 - 7 mins. Serve with Tartar Sauce.

Tartar Sauce

1 12 oz. jar of sweet/hot peppers (found in pickle section
of grocery store) - drained and minced
3 tablespoons red onion - finely minced
1/3 cup mayonnaise
1 teaspoon Old Bay Seasoning

Mix all ingredients well and refridgerate for one hour before serving.

Crab Cakes with Roasted Herbed Vegetables

Baked Rockfish topped with Crab Hollandaise and Tempura Asparagus

❦

Serves 4

This recipe combines beautifully the two iconic resources of the Rappahannock River in a most delightful way!

1 very large rockfish fillet - cut into four portions
4 tablespoons olive oil
salt and pepper
1 lb. jumbo lump crab meat
1 cup hollandaise sauce - recipe to follow
16 thin asparagus - trimmed to 4" long
1 cup tempura batter (found in Asian section of
grocery store - follow directions on box)
3 cups oil for frying
chopped parsley for garnish

Preheat to 400°
Rub rockfish filets with olive oil and salt and pepper.
Put on baking sheet and set aside.
Mix crab meat with warm hollandaise sauce and keep warm.
In a large saucepan or deep fryer heat oil to 350°.
Put asparagus into tempura batter and coat well. Fry in
batches and drain on paper towel. Keep warm.
Bake rockfish fillets in oven for eight minutes if 1" thick
- cook for sixteen minutes if 2" inch thick.

To Serve: Place rockfish on dinner plate - spoon generously with crab
hollandaise and top with tempura asparagus. Garnish with parsley.

Hollandaise Sauce

2 tablespoons white wine vinegar
2 tablespoons lemon juice
4 egg yolks - beaten well in a medium bowl
1 stick of butter - melted to foaming in a small saucepan

Combine the vinegar and the lemon juice in a microwavable
small bowl and heat for 5 seconds or until hot.
While using a hand-held blender or electric mixer, pour the hot vinegar
mixture over egg yolks while blending. Slowly stream in the hot butter
and blend until thick and smooth. Salt and pepper to taste.

**Baked Rockfish topped with Crab Hollandaise and
Tempura Asparagus served on Glorious Grits**

Herbed Rack of Lamb

༄

Serves 4

Resting the lamb after cooking assures the perfect temperature

2 Frenched Racks of Lamb
2 tablespoons finely chopped fresh rosemary
2 tablespoons finely chopped fresh thyme
salt and pepper
3 tablespoons olive oil

Pre-heat to 425°
Cut lamb racks in half, so each diner gets a four bone rack.
Rub racks of lamb with olive oil and then with fresh herbs and salt
and pepper. Place on baking sheet and roast for 10-12 mins. for
rare. Remove and allow to rest for 4-5 mins. before carving.

To serve: Holding rack with bones up - slice down
between each bone into individual chops.

Side Dishes

Braised Collard Greens

Serves 4

This recipe is a lighter version of the traditional Southern way of "cooking greens"

1 bunch of collard greens - rinsed well
2 cups vegetable broth - homemade or made from vegetable bouillion product
3 - 4 dashes of Tabasco
1/4 teaspoon liquid smoke
salt and pepper

With a sharp knife, strip out the thick stem of each collard leaf and stack leaves on top of one another. Roll the stack of leaves like a large cigar. Starting at the end cut thin, julienne strips of collards off the end of the "cigar".
In a Dutch oven, bring the boullion to a boil, add
the collards and the liquid smoke.
Cover, reduce heat and allow to simmer for 30 mins. - stirring occasionally.
Add Tabasco and allow to cook 15 mins.
Taste and adjust seasonings.

Oatmeal Souflee

∽

Serves 4

Who ever said oatmeal was a breakfast food? I love the way the texture and sweetness compliment almost any meat - especially game.

2 cups cream or half and half
1 cup quick cooking oats
4 oz. cream cheese - cut into cubes
1/2 cup maple syrup
2 eggs - seperated
candied almond topping- recipe to follow

In a medium saucepan, bring cream just to boiling point - add oats and stir. Cover and cook for five minutes or until thick. Put cream cheese into oatmeal and stir until incorporated. Add maple syrup and stir. Remove from heat and set aside.
Pre- heat oven to 350 degrees. Beat the egg whites with an electric beater until stiff. Stir egg yolks into oatmeal mixture until thick and creamy. Fold in beaten egg whites. Spoon the mixture into sprayed 4 - 6 oz. ramekins. Bake for 20-25 mins until puffy and golden. Top with candied almonds 1 min. before removing from oven. Souflee can be unmolded or left in ramekin for service.

Candied Almonds

1/3 cup light brown sugar
1 1/2 tablespoons butter
1/2 cup sliced almonds - toasted in oven till lighly golden

In a small skillet over medium heat, melt butter and add brown sugar and cook until thick and bubbly. Cook for 1-2 minutes - add almonds and stir to coat. Spread on a sprayed sheet of foil to cool and harden.

Caribbean Sweet Potatoes

∽

Serves 4

I call these potatoes "not your grandma's sweet potatoes" due to the spicy kick back!

8 medium sweet potatoes - peeled and cut into half inch cubes
1/2 cup honey
1/3 cup key lime juice
1 tablespoon cumin
3/4 teaspoon red pepper flakes - finely chopped
6 tablespoons butter

Pre-heat to 350°
In 9" x 13" pyrex casserole dish, mix the first four
ingredients with the diced sweet potatoes.
Dot with butter. Cover and bake for one hour.
Cut off off oven and uncover - allow to rest in a hot oven for 30 minutes.

Chop House Creamed Spinach

~

Serves 4

This recipe is a throwback to the 50's when the standard fare with lamb chops or a big steak in a high end chop house was creamed spinach along with a potato dish

16 ounces of fresh baby spinach
3/4 cup grated asiago cheese
1/4 cup cream
salt and pepper

In a large skillet, put the spinach in a dry pan over medium heat - allow it to just begin to wilt and reduce in size - it may be necessary to do in batches. Remove and place on paper towels. Wipe pan dry with paper towel. Add cream and bring to a boil - add cheese and whisk until smooth and creamy. Season to taste. Put spinach back into pan and mix well with cream sauce. Season again.

Zesty Greek Lemon Potatoes

⁓

Serves 4

These garlicky zippy potatoes are a natural partner for our
Herbed Rack Of Lamb - a dynamic combination!

6-8 medium red skin potatoes - strip peeled and cut into 3/4 inch cubes
1/2 cup lemon juice
1/3 cup olive oil
4 cloves garlic - smashed and minced
2 tablespoons ground oregano
salt and pepper
1 tablespoon chopped parsley
1 teaspooon lemon zest

Dry the potatoes well with paper towel. Put all the ingredients(except
parsley and lemon zest) in a large zipper bag.
Marinate in refridgerator for 1-2 days.

Pre-heat to 400°
Drain contents of bag - reserving marinade.
Place potatoes on baking sheet and roast for 30-45 mins.- stirring
occasionally. Cook until golden and slightly crispy.
In the last 5 mins of cooking, toss with reserved marinade.
Garnish with chopped parsley and lemon zest.

Roasted Kumato Tomatoes

Our local grocery store gets these lovely Kumato tomatoes which are brown in color and are sweeter than regular tomatoes - making it a perfect candidate of oven roasting. A great side dish for fish.

8-10 Kumato tomatoes - peeled and quartered
1/4 cup olive oil
salt and pepper
1/4 cup fresh chopped basil

Pre-heat to 350°
In a bowl - toss tomatoes, olive oil, salt, pepper.
Spread evenly on baking sheet and bake for 20 - 30 mins.
In the last 5 mins. of roasting - toss in chopped basil.

Herb Scalloped Potatoes

Serves 8-12

A great accompaniment to any grilled meat - we serve it for all our patio dinners

8 to 10 medium Yukon Gold potatoes - peeled, mandolined, and patted dry
1 stick butter
3 tablespoons dry Italian herbs
salt and pepper
1 1/2 cups heavy cream
2 cups grated Vermont cheddar cheese
1 teaspoon paprika

Preheat to 350°
Spray a 12 x 9 Pyrex casserole. Layer bottom of dish with
one half of the potatoes - dot with one half of the butter and
one half of the herbs. Salt and pepper generously.
Do another layer with the remaining potatoes, butter, and herbs.
Drizzle the cream over all. Cover and bake for 1 1/2 hours. Test with
fork for tenderness. Top with cheese and sprinkle with paprika. Return
to oven and bake uncovered for 15 minutes until cheese is melted.
Serve immediately.

Fabulous Fennel Corn

~

Serves 4

Everyone asks "what is that special taste in the corn?" It is that touch of fennel and a wisp of smoke that gives this side dish a unique flavor.

4 cups fresh white corn - off the cob
4 tablespoons butter
1 teaspoon of sugar
1 teaspoon of ground fennel (I grind it using a coffee bean grinder)
1/2 teaspoon cumin
1/2 teaspoon liquid smoke
1/2 cup heavy cream

Sauté corn with butter in a medium sauté pan over medium heat for 1-2 minutes. Sprinkle with sugar, fennel, cumin and liquid smoke. Stir and cook another 1 minute. Add cream and cook until thick and creamy about 4-6 minutes. Serve immediately.

Roasted Vegetable Medley

Serves 4

The key to this dish is to put the tomatoes in with the other vegetables in the final minutes of cooking

2 cups zucchini - chopped into a half a 1/2 inch dice
1 cup yellow squash - chopped into a 1/2 inch dice
3/4 cup red onion - chopped in a 1/2 inch dice
3 tablespoons olive oil
1/2 tablespoon herbes provence (or dried italian herbs)
salt and pepper
1 cup chopped tomatoes tossed with 1/2 tablespoon minced fresh thyme

Preheat to 425°
Toss the zuchinni, squash, and red onion with the olive oil. Add the herbes provence, salt and pepper and re-toss. Spread evenly on a baking sheet. Place in hot oven and roast for 8 to 10 mins.- until vegetables are beginning to brown a little. Add tomatoes to the other vegetables and allow to roast for 4-6 more minutes. Remove and stir to combine.

Glorious Grits

~

Serves 4

*These grits are made with Vermont white cheddar cheese - which creates a
cheesy creamy plate of grits - a great companion for anything on top or beside*

3 cups water
1 teaspoon salt
1 cup quick cooking grits
3/4 cup shredded Vermont Cheddar (i.e. Cabot)
4 oz. cream cheese - cut in cubes
1/4 cup cream
salt and pepper

In a medium saucepan, bring the water with the salt to a full boil. Add
grits and stir - reduce heat and cover. Allow to simmer for 5 mins. until
thick. Stir in cream cheese and cheddar until well incorporated. Add
cream - adjust seasonings. More cream can be added if needed.

Olive Oil Poached Fingerling Potatoes

༯

Serves 4

These potatoes cook completely covered in oil and
yet come out fluffy and nongreasy

16 to18 fingerling potatoes
5 cloves - crushed and minced garlic
3 to 4 cups olive oil
salt and pepper
2 tablespoons fresh rosemary - minced

Preheat to 275°
Wash the fingerlings and dry. Place in an oven proof deep dish that will hold all the potatoes snuggly. Cover with olive oil and add garlic. Cook uncovered for 45 to 60 mins. Once fork tender, remove potatoes from oil. Season salt, pepper and rosemary - sauté in hot skillet until golden.

Roasted Asparagus

~

Serves 4

The very young and very thin stalks do best for this well recieved accompaniment

Two bunches of fresh asparagus - as thin as possible and trimmed to 4" lengths
4 tablespoons olive oil
salt and pepper

Preheat to 350°
Toss asparagus with olive oil and salt and pepper and
arrange on a baking sheet. Place in hot oven for 8-10 mins.
or until just barely limp. Serve immediately.

Colonial Spoon Bread Triangles

ⁿ◦

Serves 4

Spoon Bread is a custardy Southern Dish quite often eaten with a spoon - this version is firm enough to cut into squares or triangles for easy plating and eating.

1 cup cornmeal - white preferably
1/2 cup sugar
2 teaspoons baking powder
1 teaspoon salt
1 cup boiling water
4 tablespoons butter - melted
1 cup heavy cream
1 large egg or 2 small - beaten

Pre-heat to 325°
In a bowl, combine the cornmeal, sugar, baking powder and salt. Add boiling water and melted butter and whisk until incorporated. Add cream and egg - continue to whisk until smooth. Pour into a sprayed 9"x 6" Pyrex dish and bake for 30 mins. until center is no longer jiggly and top is golden. Allow to cool slightly before cutting into triangles and spreading with honey butter (softened butter mixed with a little honey).

Curried Garden Vegetables

❧

Serves 4

This is a flavor packed side kick for either chicken or pork

1/4 cup olive oil
1 cup chopped broccoli
1/2 cup chopped celery
1 cup chopped onion
1 cup chopped peppers - yellow and/or red
1 cup chopped zucchini
4 cloves garlic - smashed and minced
2 cups chopped tomatoes
1 cup sliced mushrooms
2 tablespoons grated ginger
1 tablespoon ground thyme
1 tablespoon ground oregano
1 teaspoon curry powder
1 teaspoon cumin
2 cups vegetable stock
1 tablespoon cornstarch mixed with 3 tablespoons water

In a large skillet, sauté all the vegetables except the mushrooms
and tomatoes in olive oil until just soft but still crunchy.
Add tomatoes and mushrooms and all the seasonings. Stir to mix.
Add vegetable stock and cook until bubbly. Stir in cornstarch
mixture and stir until thick. Serve while vegetables or still crisp.

Orzo Primavera

⌒

Serves 4

I love serving this pasta side with chicken or veal piccata

2 cups orzo (rice shaped pasta)
4 tablespoons olive oil
salt and pepper
1 cup asparagus tips - 2 inches long
one dozen cherry tomatoes
1 cup red onion - chopped in 1/2 inch dice
1/2 cup sliced black olives
1/4 chopped fresh herbs - oregano, basil, and thyme
2/3 cup finely grated Romano cheese

In a saucepan of boiling water, cook orzo until tender. Drain and return
to pan and toss with 2 tablespoons olive oil. Salt and pepper to taste.

Preheat to 400°
In remaining 2 tablespoons of olive oil, toss asparagus tips, red onions, and
cherry tomatoes. Salt and pepper liberally. Spread vegetables on a baking
sheet and oven roast for 6 - 8 minutes or until vegetables are crisp/tender.
Combine roasted vegetables and orzo - add olives, chopped
herbs, and cheese - toss well. Salt and pepper to taste

Puréed Parsnips with Horseradish

∽

Serves 4

Parsnips are an easily forgotten vegetable but with the added zing of horseradish - they become memorable!

4 cups parsnips - peeled and cut into chunks
(I cut out the woody middle part)
4 tablespoons butter
3 tablespoons jarred horseradish
salt and pepper

Place 1 inch of water in a large saucepan. Add parsnips and cover. Cook on medium high heat until parsnips are fork tender. Drain and mash - add butter and horseradish and mash well, using a potato masher. Salt and pepper to taste.

Sweet and Sour Butternut Squash

⁓

Serves 4

The sweet/sour sensation makes "can be boring" butternut squash pop with flavor!

4 cups butternut squash - peeled and cut into fingers
2 cups vidalia or sweet onion - sliced thin or mandolined
1/4 cup olive oil
2 cloves garlic - smashed and minced
1 tablespoon cumin
2 tablespoon cilantro - chopped
1/2 cup water
1/2 cup golden raisins
4 tablespoons butter
2 tablespoons sherry vinegar
2 tablespoons balsamic vinegar
3 tablespoons sugar

Sauté squash and onions in olive oil until onions are translucent
- add garlic, cumin, cilantro and water. Cover and allow to
cook for 8 to 10 minutes over medium high heat.
Uncover - add raisins, butter, vinegars and sugar. Cook until thick and glazed.

Savory Mushroom Bread Pudding

❦

Serves 4

This makes a nice accompaniment for Prime Rib or any other roasted meats

2 cups dense / rustic type bread - crust removed
1/2 cup cream
2 eggs - beaten
1/2 cup vegetable stock
3 cups chopped mushrooms - assorted if you like
salt and pepper

Preheat to 350°
In a bowl, combine all ingredients and allow to sit for 20 minutes.
Spoon into a sprayed pyrex casserole and bake for one hour.

Blue Cheese and Broccolini Souflee

༄

Serves 4

An unusual twist for a side - especially good with grilled steak

4 cups broccolini - cooked and chopped coarsely
1 large egg - beaten
1/2 cup blue cheese crumbles
3 tablespoons Greek yogurt or sour cream

Preheat to 425°
Mix all ingredients well and spoon into a sprayed small casserole or individual ramekins. Bake for 15 to 20 minutes until puffy and beginning to brown.

Braised Savoy Cabbage

∾

Serves 4

The key to this savory side is the addition of lots of butter at the finish

6 cups shredded Savoy cabbage (Bok Choy can be substituted)
4 tablespoons olive oil
1/4 cup Worcestershire sauce
4 tablespoons butter
salt-and-pepper

In a skillet, saute cabbage in olive oil over medium high. When wilted, add Worcestershire and cover. Cook for 10 to 15 minutes until tender. Just before serving - add butter and salt and pepper to taste.

Asparagus Flan with Fontina Cheese Sauce

Serves 4

An elegant and rich addition to any meal

1 cup chopped onion
2 tablespoons olive oil
2 tablespoons butter
2 cups cooked asparagus - cut into 1" pieces
1 cup cream
3 eggs - beaten
1 cup grated Parmesan cheese
salt-and-pepper
1/2 cup fontina cheese sauce - recipe to follow
parsley sprigs

Preheat to 300°
In a skillet, sauté onion in olive oil and butter until opaque. Add
asparagus and cream and cook for 10 minutes. Allow to cool slightly.
Pour into food processor and whir for 20 seconds - until well blended.
In a bowl combine eggs, parmesan cheese, and processed asparagus mixture.
Salt and pepper to taste Mix well. Spoon into buttered individual ramekins
and place in hot water bath - cover loosely with
foil and bake 30 minutes or until set.

To serve: Run a knife around sides of ramekin to loosen flan.
Invert onto plate and shake gently to unmold flan. Drizzle with
fontina cheese sauce and garnish with parsley sprigs.

Fontina Cheese Sauce

1 cup grated fontina cheese
1/2 cup cream
1/4 teaspoon ground thyme
1/4 teaspoon nutmeg

In a small saucepan, heat all ingredients and whisk until hot and smooth.

Desserts

Key Lime Mousse with Agave Marinated Berries

Serves 4

This light and airy dessert is the perfect ending for a summer dinner

3 cups heavy whipping cream
3/4 cup sugar
4 tablespoons key lime juice - key lime juice is best,
but regular lime juice can be used

Combine cream and sugar in a bowl and beat with an electric mixer and until it begins to stiffen - slowly add key lime juice while continuing to beat until cream is thick and almost curdly. Refridgerate until use.

To serve: Spoon Lime Mousse into martini glasses and top each with 6-8 marinated berries. Garnish with a mint sprig.

Agave Marinated Berries
2 tablespoons sugar
4 tablespoons water
1/4 cup agave tequila
1 pint fresh blackberries
1 pint fresh rasberries

Combine the sugar and the water in a microwavable bowl and heat in microwave until hot. Stir until sugar is dissolved. Add tequila and stir - allow to cool before adding the berries - mix to coat well, and refridgerate for two to three hours.

Key Lime Mousse with Agave Marinated Berries

Carribean Rum Poke Cake with Tropical Fruit Cream

This recipe evokes visions of palm trees, teal waters, and reggae music!

2 sticks butter
3 cups sugar
1 cup sour cream
1/2 teaspoon baking soda
3 cups flour
6 eggs
1 teaspoon vanilla
1 teaspoon rum or coconut extract
Buttered Rum Sauce - recipe to follow
Tropical Fruit Cream - recipe to follow
mint sprigs

Preheat to 325°
In a large bowl, cream the butter and sugar together until fluffy. Add sour cream and mix well. Add 1/2 of the flour and mix - add 3 eggs and mix until incorporated. Finish with the rest of the flour, the baking soda and the flavorings. Mix well.
Pour into a greased Pyrex baking dish - 13"x 9" or so- and bake for 1 hr. and 15 minutes until tester comes out clean.
After removing from oven allow cake to cool slightly, but while still warm, poke holes deep into the cake with a chop stick. Pour warm rum sauce into holes to saturate cake. Cover and set aside.

To serve: Cut cake into 3 inch squares and top with several dollops of the fruit cream. Garnish with mint sprig and powdered sugar.

Buttered Rum Sauce

2 sticks butter
1 cup sugar
4 tablespoons of water
1/2 cup dark rum

In a medium saucepan over medium heat, melt the butter - add sugar and water and cook - stirring until smooth and bubbly. Continue to cook for 2 minutes. Remove from heat and slowly add rum while stirring. Continue to stir until rum is well incorporated.

Tropical Fruit Cream

2 cups heavy cream
1/2 cup sugar
2 tablespoons lime juice
1/4 teaspoon orange extract
3 cups cut up assorted fresh fruit - strawberries, pineapple, peaches, mangoes, berries etc.
3 tablespoons honey

In a large bowl, combine the heavy cream and sugar and beat with an electric beater. Add orange extract just before cream has reached heavy whipped cream stage. Refridgerate until ready to use. Mix fresh fruit with honey and refridgerate.

At serving time: Combine fruit with cream and mix gently.

Chocolate Decadence with Rasberry Coulis

∾

Serves 10

This epic flourless cake from the eighties does very well
being prepared several days in advance

12 ounces semi sweet chocolate morsels
1 1/2 sticks butter
4 large eggs
1/2 cup sugar
rasberry coulis sauce - recipe to follow
whipped cream garnish
fresh rasberries

Preheat to 350°
Butter and flour an 8x8 pryex dish.
Melt chocolate and butter in a metal bowl, set over a saucepan
of simmering water, whisking until smooth. Set aside.
In a large bowl beat together eggs and sugar with
electric beater until lemony - about 7-8 mins.
Slowly fold egg mixture into chocolate and stir until well incorporated.
Pour into prepared pan and place in water bath and bake 45 mins.or until top
is set. Cool completely and refridgerate for 4 or more hours before unmolding.

To serve: Run knife around edge of pan - place pan on stove burner over
low heat and move pan around to heat entire bottom. Invert cake on
cutting board - prying it out with knife tip if necessary. Cut into triangles.
Place triangle on dessert plate - garnish with rasberry coulis,
whipped cream, fresh rasberries and mint sprig.

Rasberry Coulis

10 ounce bag of frozen rasberries-thawed
1/4 cup sugar

Put rasberries and sugar in a food processor and whir - force through a fine sieve to remove seeds. Pour into squirt bottle.

Chocolate Decadence with Rasberry Coulis

Key Lime Panna Cotta with Lingonberry Coulis

∽

Serves 4

Cool and refreshing - this makes a wonderful respite after a sumptuous meal

3 tablespoons water
2 envelopes gelatin
4 cups heavy cream
1/2 cup sugar
2 teaspoons vanilla extract
1 teaspoon grated lime zest
1 tablespoon Key lime juice
Lingonberry coulis - recipe to follow
cut lime for garnish
mint sprigs

Put water into a medium bowl and sprinkle gelatin
over top - allow to stand for five minutes.
In a medium saucepan over medium heat, combine cream
and sugar - cook until sugar is dissolved. Remove from
heat and stir in vanilla, lime zest, and lime juice.
Pour warm cream mixture over gelatin stir until dissolved.
Pour cream mixture into four individual ramekins or coffee cups that
have been sprayed with Pam. Refrigerate for three to four hours.

To Serve: Run a knife around ramekins to loosen Panna
Cotta. Invert onto dessert plate - drizzle with lingonberry
sauce and garnish with lime twist and mint.

Lingonberry Coulis

1 jar lingonberry preserves
1 tablespoon lime juice

Heat preserves in a saucepan until melted. Add lime juice -
allow to cool slightly and whir in food processor until smooth.
Pour into a squirt bottle and refrigerate until needed.

Blueberry Bread Pudding With Rum Sauce

∽

Serves 8

This timeless classic never loses its appeal - a true comfort food

1 loaf cinnamon raisin bread - torn into small pieces
3/4 quart milk
1 stick of butter- melted
4 tablespoons vanilla
5 eggs - beaten
2 cups sugar
pinch of salt
1 pint fresh blueberries
Rum Sauce - recipe to follow
mint sprigs

Pre-heat to 350 degrees
Soak the torn bread in the milk for 15 minutes. Add
remaining ingredients and mix well.
Pour into sprayed 8"x11" pan and bake for about
one hour until tester comes out clean.

To serve: Cut pudding into squares and top with rum sauce.
Garnish with mint and sprinkle with powdered sugar.

Rum Sauce

1 cup heavy cream
1 cup confectioners sugar
2 tablespoons cornstarch dissolved in 4 tablespoons of water
1/2 cup of rum

In a medium saucepan over medium heat, combine the cream
and the sugar, whisking until bubbly and smooth.
Add dissolved corn starch, cooking and stirring until
thick. Remove from heat and add rum.

Chocolate Raspberry Tiramisu Parfait

Serves 4

A fun remake of the Italian dessert of the 80s

1/3 cup espresso or very strong coffee
1/4 cup brandy
4 large slices pound cake - cut into 1 inch cubes
8 ounces softened cream cheese
1 3/4 cup heavy cream
1/2 cup sugar
3 tablespoons fudge sauce - the kind used for ice cream sundaes
1 pint raspberries
1/3 cup Chambord or any raspberry liqueur
1 teaspoon cocoa powder
1/8 teaspoon ground cloves

Mix together espresso and brandy. Spread pound cake cubes on a large plate and sprinkle with espresso mixture - soaking each cube. In a medium bowl, beat the cream cheese,1/2 cup cream,1/4 cup sugar, and fudge sauce together until smooth and creamy. In a small bowl, combine raspberries and Chambord. Set aside. In a small bowl, beat the remaining cream and the remaining sugar to a firm whip cream.

To assemble: In the bottom of a wide mouth wineglass - spoon one quarter of the soaked pound cake cubes. Top with one quarter of the chocolate mixture, then a layer of the raspberries. Top with a huge dollop of whipped cream dusted with a mixture of cocoa powder and ground cloves. Garnish with mint sprigs.

Chocolate Rasberry Tiramisu Parfait

Apple Tart Tartin

Serves 4

I teach this recipe in our French Provincial cooking class - my students feel a real sense of accomplishment by cooking and serving this classic French dessert

1 stick butter
1 cup sugar
8 peeled and quartered granny smith apples
1 sheet frozen puff pastry - rolled and cut to fit your
tart dish - allowing a 1 inch overhang
4 tablespoons vanilla yogurt, whipped cream, or crème fraîche
Mint sprigs

Preheat to 400°
In a medium saucepan, over medium heat; combine butter and sugar - cook at a steady bubble - stirring often with a whisk until mixture is a dark amber color - about 10 to 15 minutes. Pour into bottom of an 8 inch Pyrex tart dish or cake pan.
Arrange apple pieces on top of caramel - flat side down - crowd the dish, the apples shrink a lot during cooking. Add a second layer if needed. Bake for 20 to 25 minutes. Remove and gently place puff pastry on top of the apples and tuck in edges to form rim. Prick top with air holes and return to oven to bake until pastry is puffy and brown - about 15 minutes. Remove and cool slightly.

To Serve: Run a knife around the outside edge of tart. Invert onto a serving platter by putting the serving platter on the top of the tart dish - hold both dishes securely and give a quick flip. Allow to cool slightly - cut into wedges and serve alongside a dollop of crème fraîche, whipped cream or my favorite - vanilla yogurt!
Garnish with mint sprigs

Bananas Foster Flambe

Serves 4

It is fun to bring this out from the kitchen - flaming - into a dim dining room to be spooned over waiting bowls of ice cream

1/2 cup brown sugar
4 tablespoons butter
1 tablespoon heavy cream
4 bananas, cut on diagonal
1/3 cup shredded coconut (optional)
1/2 cup dark rum - warmed
4 servings rum raisin ice cream

In a medium skillet over medium heat, melt butter. Add brown sugar, whisk and cook until smooth. Add cream and stir - add bananas and heat for one minute. Sprinkle with coconut - add rum (do not stir). Ignite rum.(Rum must warm for it to ignite).

To serve: Spoon flaming bananas over ice cream.

Sticky Toffee Pudding with Caramel Sauce

∽

Serves 8-10

This recipe is one of our most requested - it is the quintessential comfort dessert- warm, and delicately gooey then coupled with ice cream - it is sheer heaven!

8 ounces dates,chopped
1 cup boiling water
1 stick of butter- room temperature
1 cup of light brown sugar
4 eggs
1 3/4 cups flour
1 tablespoon instant coffee
1 teaspoon baking soda
Toffee Sauce - recipe to follow
1 cup sweetened whipped cream
2 cups french vanilla bean ice cream

Preheat to 350°
Butter and flour a 9" x 13" pyrex dish.
Place dates in a bowl and cover with boiling water. Set aside.
Beat butter and sugar with an electric mixer until blended.
Add 2 eggs - beat well - add 1/2 the flour. Add the last two
eggs, and the remaining flour and blend well.
Add coffee and baking soda to the date mixture.
Add date mixture to batter and mix well.
Pour batter into prepared pan and bake approximately 40
mins. until tester comes out clean. Allow to cool slightly.
While cake is still warm, poke holes with the end of a wooden spoon every 2-3
inches of the surface of the cake - all the way through to the bottom of the cake.

Pour warm caramel sauce into the holes and around the edges, reserving 1/2 cup of sauce. Cover and allow cake to sit several hours before cutting.

To serve: On a dessert plate, pool 2 tablespoons of
sauce and place a cut square of cake on top.
Top with sweetened whip cream and a side of vanilla ice cream.
Garnish with a mint sprig and powdered sugar.

Caramel Sauce

1 stick of butter
2 1/2 cups light brown sugar
1/2 cup cream

Melt butter in a medium saucepan over medium heat.
Add sugar and whisk until incorporated.
Add cream and whisk until smooth, hot and bubbly.

Puff Pastry Napoleons with Fresh Fruit Creme

Serves 4

*A true experience in decadence - conjures up visions
of Arc de Triomphe and the Eiffel!*

1/3 cup sugar
1 tablespoon cornstarch
3/4 cup cream
2 egg yolks - beaten
1/2 tablespoon butter
2 teaspoons vanilla extract
Frozen puff pastry sheet - thawed and cut into 4 inch squares
Fresh Fruit Creme - recipe to follow

In a small saucepan over medium heat, combine sugar and cornstarch.
Add cream, cook and whisk until bubbly. Remove from heat. Add a
tablespoon of the hot mixture to the egg yolks and mix well. Continue
to combine hot mixture and egg yolks until all is well incorporated.
Return to medium heat and continue stirring while it comes to a gentle
boil. Allow to boil for 1 minute. Remove from heat and stir in butter
and vanilla extract. Cover and refrigerate for at least two hours.
Preheat to 350°
Place puff pastry squares on baking sheet and bake 10 to 15
minutes until golden and puffy. Allow to cool - slice horizontally
in half and remove excess loose dough. Set aside.

To serve: Spoon four tablespoons of custard into bottom half of puff
pastry square. Top with fresh fruit creme and then cap with top half of puff
pastry. Garnish with strawberry fan and sprinkle with powdered sugar.

Fresh Fruit Creme

2 cups heavy cream
1/4 cup sugar
3 cups fresh fruit - cut into pieces and sprinkled lightly with sugar

In a bowl, beat cream and sugar with an electric
mixer until stiff and thick. Fold in fruit.

Puff Pastry Napoleon with Fresh Fruit Creme

Baked Pears with Brie Cheese in Caramel Sauce

Serves 4

ohh! The sweetness of the pears and creaminess of the Brie - all in a pool of caramel!

2 tablespoons butter
3/4 cup brown sugar
3 tablespoons heavy cream
2 pears - peeled, halved, and cored
1/2 lb. Brie cheese - rind removed and cut into four pieces
mint sprigs

Preheat to 375°
Place butter in a small skillet over medium heat. When melted, add brown
sugar and whisk until smooth and hot. Add cream and lower heat.
Bake pears for 8 to 10 minutes, until fork tender. Remove.
Place one piece of cheese in the core of the halved baked
pear and return to oven until cheese begins to melt.

To serve: Pool warm caramel sauce on a small plate and place pear in middle.
Drizzle with more sauce - garnish with mint sprigs and powdered sugar.

Baked Pear with Brie Cheese in Caramel Sauce

Breakfast and Brunch

Croissant French Toast with Strawberry Balsamic Syrup and Vanilla Yogurt Drizzle

Serves 4

The velvet texture of the croissant soothes the edginess of the balsamic as it carries you into sweetness of the yogurt - a journey of delight for one's palate!

4 large croissants - cut in half
2 eggs
1/2 cup cream
2 teaspoons vanilla
2 tablespoons sugar
4 tablespoons butter
1 1/2 cups balsamic vinegar
1/3 cup sugar
2 cups sliced strawberries
4 tablespoons softened butter
1/2 cup vanilla yogurt - spooned into a squirt bottle
mint sprigs

Whisk together the eggs, cream, vanilla, and sugar. Dip croissant half into egg mixture and soak for 10 seconds. In a skillet melt butter and sauté croissants until golden.
In a saucepan, combine balsamic vinegar and sugar. Cook over medium high heat until reduced by half. Add strawberries and heat slightly.

To serve: Place croissant on plate - lavish with softened butter and spoon strawberries overtop. Drizzle with yogurt and garnish with mint.

Croissant French Toast with Strawberry Balsamic Syrup and Sweet Yogurt Drizzle

Huevos Rancheros a la Summer Duck

∽

Serves 4

*Add a tequila sunrise cocktail to this zesty remake of the
Mexican classic and say Ole to your Sunday brunch!*

1 can Pinto beans - drained
1/2 cup chicken stock
1/3 cup jarred vindaloo sauce or curry sauce
4 six-inch flour tortillas
1/4 cup oil
2 avocados - sliced
8 eggs - softly scrambled and kept warm
8 slices queso fresco (soft Mexican cheese found
in cheese section of grocery store)
1/4 teaspoon smoked paprika
2 cups fresh salsa - recipe to follow
1 cup sour cream

Heat broiler.
In a bowl, mash pinto beans with chicken stock, add curry
sauce and mix well. Heat in microwave until hot.
Fry tortillas in oil until crispy - drain on paper towels.
On a baking sheet, place tortillas - top with 2 tablespoons bean mixture then
a layer of sliced avocado - then a serving of scrambled eggs - top with sliced
queso fresco. Run under broiler to melt cheese. Sprinkle with smoked paprika.

To serve: Plate Huevos Rancheros and surround with salsa and
dollops of sour cream. Garnish with cilantro leaves.

Fresh Salsa

2 cups chopped tomatoes
1/2 cup chopped onions
2 tablespoons chopped jalapenos
1 clove garlic - smashed and minced
1 tablespoon lime juice
3 tablespoons chopped cilantro
salt and pepper

In a bowl, combine all ingredients.

Southern Sausage Gravy Over Sun-Dried Tomato Biscuits

Serves 4

*Marry this with a serving of cheesy soft scrambled eggs
and you have a real Southern treat for brunch*

2 cups biscuit mix
2/3 cup buttermilk
1/4 cup finely minced onion
1/4 cup finely chopped sun-dried tomatoes

6 tablespoons butter
3 tablespoons flour
2 cups cream
1 tablepoon Worcestershire sauce
1 tablespoon beef bouillon paste or 1/2 cup beef stock
1 lb. bulk breakfast sausage - browned and drained
1 teaspoon ground sage
1 teaspoon ground thyme
salt and pepper
thyme sprigs

Pre-heat to 400°
Combine biscuit mix and buttermilk. Add onions and sun-
dried tomatoes - knead lightly and roll out to 3/4 inch
thickness. Cut out 3 inch biscuits and bake until golden.

Melt 4 tablespoons butter in skillet over medium heat - sprinkle with flour and whisk until incorporated. Add one half of the cream and whisk until thick. Add remaining cream, whisking until creamy. Add bouillon paste and Worcestershire. Salt-and-pepper to taste. Add cooked sausage, sage and thyme and stir to mix.

To serve: Split hot biscuit and spread with softened butter. Spoon sausage gravy on top and garnish with thyme sprigs.

Buttermilk Pancake Tower with Pulled Pork Barbecue and Jack Daniels Syrup

∽

Serves 4

Sound crazy? It is! But the taste sensation is unbelievable!!

2 cups baking mix
2 eggs
2 tablespoons melted butter
1 1/4 cups buttermilk
2 cups pulled pork - lightly sauced and warm
2 cups Jack Daniels syrup - recipe to follow

Combine baking mix, eggs, melted butter, and buttermilk. Heat up a greased griddle or skillet and ladle batter for pancakes onto griddle - Cook until golden and done through.

To serve: On a plate, alternate layers of pancake and pork barbecue to form a tower and drizzle generously with syrup.

Jack Daniels Syrup

3 tablespoons butter
1 cup water
1 cup brown sugar
1/2 cup sugar
1/2 cup Jack Daniels bourbon

In a saucepan, combine all ingredients over medium heat and cook until thick and syrupy.

Buttermilk Pancakes with Pulled Pork Bar-B-Q and Jack Daniels Syrup

The Ultimate Continental Breakfast

∽

Serves 4

Classic melon and proscuitto together with French Pain Au Chocolate and Almond Croissants - C'est tres bon!

8 cantaloupe slices
1/2 lb. proscuitto
4 frozen puff pastry sheets
1 cup semi sweet chocolate morsels
1 can almond paste (found in the baking section of grocery store)
1/4 cup melted butter
1/2 cup sliced almonds - toasted
2 tablespoons mint jelly
1/3 cup vanilla yogurt
confectioners sugar
fresh mint sprigs

Preheat to 400°
Arrange cantaloupe slices and prosciutto decoratively on a plate. Set aside.
Cut four triangles with a 4" base and eight 4" squares from the
puff pastry sheets. On four of the squares place 2 tablespoons
chocolate morsels. Top with another square. Seal edges.
On each triangle, spread one tablespoon of almond paste. Starting
at the base, roll up like a croissant turning in edges at the finish.
Place almond croissants and pain au chocolate on sprayed baking pan and bake
until puffy and golden. Brush pastries with butter. Top croissants with almonds.

Combine mint jelly and yogurt in a squirt bottle and shake vigorously.

To serve: On the cantaloupe platter, arrange the pastries and dust with confectioners sugar. Garnish with squiggles from yogurt and mint mixture and fresh mint.

The Ultimate Continental Breakfast

Duck Hash over Sweet Griddle Cakes

Serves 4

My father would make this after a good day of duck hunting - it continues to be a family favorite !

1 fresh or frozen (thawed) duck - cut into 4 parts
1 cup chopped carrots
1 cup chopped onions
1 stick butter
1/2 cup flour
2 cups beef stock
1 cup red wine
1/3 cup Worcestershire sauce
3/4 tablespoon ground thyme
salt and pepper
1 package corn muffin mix
1 egg
2 tablespoons melted butter
3/4 cup milk
1/2 cup sugar
thyme sprigs

Place duck parts into Dutch oven cover with water. Add vegetables, cover and simmer two hours or until duck begins to fall off the bone. Remove from water and cool. Pull duck meat from bones . Set aside.

In a skillet, melt butter- sprinkle with flour and stir. Whisk in beef stock and whisk until thick and smooth. Add red wine, Worcestershire, and thyme - stir until incorporated. Salt and pepper to taste. Add duck meat and cook for 10 minutes.

Combine corn muffin mix with egg, melted butter, milk, and sugar. Ladle 3 -4 ounces mixture onto a hot greased griddle or skillet to make griddle cakes and cook on both sides until golden.

To serve: Place a stack of 4 griddle cakes on a plate and slather with butter. Spoon Duck Hash over top and garnish with thyme sprigs.

Croque Madame - Parisian Style

❡

Serves 4

While in cooking school in Paris -- this was my daily sustenance. The salad is an integral part - don't skip it - even for breakfast!

4 tablespoons mayonnaise
6 tablespoons mustard - dijon or a grain mustard
8 slices rustic French bread
1/2 lb. cooked ham - thinly sliced
2 cups grated Gruyere cheese
4 tablespoons softened butter
4 eggs - cooked sunny side up or over easy
Parisian salad - recipe follows

Heat broiler. Mix mayonnaise and 2 tablespoons mustard. Set aside.
Spread one side of bread with one tablespoon mustard only. Top with a layer of ham and 1/4 cup cheese. (Reserve 1 cup of cheese) Top with other bread slice.
Spread both sides sandwich with soft butter.
In a skillet or griddle, cook sandwiches over medium heat
until golden and cheese is beginning to melt.
Place sandwiches on a baking sheet - spread top of each sandwich with mayonnaise/mustard mixture and 1/4 cup cheese. Broil until hot and bubbly.

To serve: Top each sandwich with cooked egg
and serve salad nestled alongside.

Parisian Salad

1/2 cup olive oil
1/4 cup red wine vinegar
1 teaspoon Cavender's Greek seasoning
2 cups mixed herb greens

Combine oil, vinegar, seasoning in a jar and shake well (you will have left over dressing). Toss appropriate amount of dressing with greens.

Croque Madame with Parisian Salad

Gingerbread Waffles with Sweet Peach Chutney And Clove Whipped Cream

～

Serves 4

Does this say Christmas morning or what??

2 cups baking mix
1 cup milk
2 eggs - beaten
1/2 cup brown sugar
1/3 cup molasses
1/2 cup sweet potato purée - canned or left over
3 teaspoons ground ginger
2 teaspoons cinnamon
1/4 teaspoons nutmeg
2 cups Peach Chutney Sauce - recipe follows
1 cup sweetened whipped cream
1/8 teaspoon ground cloves

In a large bowl, combine all ingredients (except chutney) and mix well with a hand-held mixer. Pour batter into preheated waffle iron and cook until golden.

To serve: Place waffle on plate and top with a generous dollop of peach chutney and spoonful of sweetened whipped cream sprinkled with ground cloves.

Peach Chutney:

2 jars Indian chutney
2 cups fresh peaches - chopped (use canned in a pinch)
1/3 cup pomegranate syrup (or any fruit syrup)

Combine all ingredients in a saucepan and heat until thick and syrupy.

Krispy Kreme Donut French Toast with Triple Berry Devonshire Creme

~

Serves 4

The inner child in all of us cries out in joy when this is placed in front of them!

8 glazed doughnuts - preferably day old
2 eggs - beaten
1/2 cup cream
1 teaspoons vanilla
1 tablespoon sugar
4 tablespoons butter
2 cups triple berry cream - recipe to follow
mint sprigs

Slice doughnuts horizontally - set aside.
In a medium bowl combine eggs, cream, vanilla, and sugar.
Over medium heat melt butter in a large skillet or griddle.
Dip doughnut into egg mixture and sauté until golden brown.

To serve: Place doughnut halves on plate and top with a generous dollop of
Triple Berry Devonshire cream. Garnish with powdered sugar and mint sprigs.

Triple Berry Devonshire Cream

1/2 cup sour cream or creme fraiche
1/2 cup heavy whipping cream
2 tablespoons sugar
2 cups mixed fresh berries - (strawberries, raspberries,
blueberries, blackberries etc.)

In a bowl, combine sour cream,cream and sugar- beat
with an electric mixer to soft peaks. Fold in fruit.

Eggs a la Anne

⌒

Serves 4

This is my version of Eggs Benedict - it is a great dish to serve on New Year's day after a late night of ringing in the New Year.

4-8 slices of green or "pink" tomatoes
1 egg - beaten
1/2 cup panko breadcrumbs
2 cups frying oil
1/2 lb. thinly sliced country ham
2 tablespoons butter
4 eggs
salt-and-pepper
2 English muffins - split, buttered and toasted
1 cup grated Vermont cheddar cheese
1 cup Easy Bearnaise Sauce - recipe to follow
smoked paprika
chopped parsley

Dip slices of tomato into egg then into breadcrumbs. Heat oil to 350° and fry tomato slices until crispy and golden - keep warm. Sauté ham in butter until edges begin to curl - keep warm. Sauté four eggs over easy - season with salt and pepper.

To Assemble: Heat broiler. Place English muffin half on a baking pan and top with a few ham slices, then fried tomato slices - followed by an egg. Sprinkle top with 2 tablespoons grated cheese and a shake of paprika. Broil until cheese is melted.

To serve: Place an Egg a la Anne on a plate and spoon Bearnaise sauce over top. Garnish with chopped parsley.

Easy Bearnaise Sauce

1 stick butter - cut up
1 tablespoon lemon juice
1 tablespoon white wine vinegar
1 tablespoon dried tarragon
2 large egg yolks - beaten
pinch of cayenne

Combine all ingredients in a saucepan over low heat. Whisk until butter melts and then constantly whisk until thick.

Index

Grilled Pear Salad with Herbed Goat Cheese, Candied Pecans, Dried Blueberries, and a Peach Balsamic Dressing, 48

Tower Beet Salad with Fig Balsamic Dressing, 50

Chopped Salad with Classic Green Goddess Dressing, 51

Wedge of Romaine with Tiny Tim Tomatoes, Mandolined Onions, Crispy Bacon and Blue Cheese Dressing, 54

Our Classic Caesar Salad, 56

Watermelon Salad with Feta and Mint Dressing, 58

Entrees - 61

Duck Breast with Cherries in Port Wine Sauce, 62

Chicken Cordon Bleu with Dijonnaise Sauce, 64

Grilled Jumbo Shrimp And Grits, 66

Pan Seared Scallops with Buerre Blanc and Mustard-Honey Dapple, 68

Pan Seared Salmon with Capers, Shallots, and Lemon Sauce served atop Spinach Colcannon, 70

French Countryside Cassoulet, 72

Chateaubriand with Roquefort Sauce, 74

Slow Braised Short Ribs On a Rosemary and Thyme Potato Mash surrounded by a Roasted Root Vegetables, 76

Glory, Glory Crab Cakes with Amen Tartar Sauce, 78

Baked Rockfish topped with Crab Hollandaise and Tempura Asparagus, 80

Herbed Rack of Lamb, 82

Sides - 85

Braised Collard Greens, 86

Oatmeal Souflee, 87

Caribbean Sweet Potatoes, 88

Chop House Creamed Spinach, 89

Zesty Greek Lemon Potatoes, 90

Roasted Kumato Tomatoes, 91

Herb Scalloped Potatoes, 92

Fabulous Fennel Corn, 93

Roasted Vegetable Medley, 94

Glorious Grits, 95

Olive Oil Poached Fingerling Potatoes, 96